Voices for Green Choices

David Suzuki

Doing Battle with Climate Change

By Suzy Gazlay

Crabtree Publishing Company

www.crabtreebooks.com

Crabtree Publishing Company

Author: Suzy Gazlay
Publishing plan research and development:
   Sean Charlebois, Reagan Miller
   Crabtree Publishing Company
Editor: Lynn Peppas
Proofreader: Crystal Sikkens
Project coordinator: Robert Walker
Content and curriculum adviser: Suzy Gazlay, M.A.
Editorial: Mark Sachner
Photo research: Ruth Owen
Design: Westgraphix/Tammy West
Production coordinator: Margaret Amy Salter
Prepress technicians: Margaret Amy Salter, Ken Wright

Written, developed, and produced by Water Buffalo Books

Cover photo: The amount of seawater, plus the contrast between the color of this polar bear and its surroundings, indicates a serious problem. The bear should be blending in with an icy, snowy habitat. Sadly, climate change is causing the polar ice caps to melt, endangering this bear and its relatives.

Photo credits:
Alamy: Chris Cheadle: page 13 (top)
The Canadian Press: Darryl Dyck: page 31 (bottom);
   Fred Chartrand: page 42 (bottom)
CBC Still Photo Collection: pages 20 (top), 24 (top)
Corbis: page 10 (bottom); Joel W. Rogers: page 5 (bottom);
   Bettmann: pages 8 (left), 9 (top); Orban Thierry:
   page 36 (bottom)
George Douklias: cover (inset), pages 1, 23 (left), 27 (left)
FLPA: Flip Nicklin: page 38 (bottom)
Getty Images: Alfred Eisenstaedt: page 17 (bottom);
   Popperfoto: page 19 (left); FPG Hulton Archive:
   page 22 (top); Gerard Cerles: page 30 (top); Luis Liwanag:
   page 40 (top); Manpreet Romana: page 40 (bottom)
John W. MacDonald: pages 4 (left), 15 (bottom)
Parks Canada National Photo Collection/ NP/W. Lynch/image
   11Q: page 26 (bottom)
Royal BC Museum, BC Archives: Image i60959: page 12 (top)
Science Photo Library: A. Barrington Brown: page 16 (left);
   Klaus Guldbrands: page 29 (top)
Shutterstock: cover (main), pages 6, 7, 13 (center and
   bottom), 18 (top), 25 (bottom), 27, 28, 32 (left), 33, 34,
   35, 39 (right), 41
University of Washington Libraries: page 11 (right)

Library and Archives Canada Cataloguing in Publication

Gazlay, Suzy
   David Suzuki : doing battle with climate change / Suzy Gazlay.

(Voices for green choices)
Includes index.
ISBN 978-0-7787-4665-2 (bound).--ISBN 978-0-7787-4678-2 (pbk.)

   1. Suzuki, David, 1936- --Juvenile literature. 2. Global
warming--Juvenile literature. 3. Climatic changes--Juvenile literature. 4. Environmentalists--Canada--Biography--Juvenile literature.
5. Broadcasters--Canada--Biography--Juvenile literature.
I. Title. II. Series: Voices for green choices

GE56.S89G39 2009   j333.72092   C2009-900159-4

Library of Congress Cataloging-in-Publication Data

Gazlay, Suzy.
   David Suzuki : doing battle with climate change / by Suzy
Gazlay.
       p. cm. -- (Voices for green choices)
   Includes index.
   ISBN 978-0-7787-4678-2 (pbk. : alk. paper)
-- ISBN 978-0-7787-4665-2 (reinforced library binding : alk. paper)
   1. Suzuki, David T., 1936---Juvenile literature.
   2. Environmentalists--United States--Biography--Juvenile
literature. I. Title.

GE56.S8G39 2009
333.72092--dc22
[B]
                                          2008055883

Crabtree Publishing Company

www.crabtreebooks.com   1-800-387-7650

Published in Canada
Crabtree Publishing
616 Welland Ave.
St. Catharines, Ontario
L2M 5V6

Published in the United States
Crabtree Publishing
PMB16A
350 Fifth Ave., Suite 3308
New York, NY 10118

Published in the United Kingdom
Crabtree Publishing
White Cross Mills
High Town, Lancaster
LA1 4XS

Published in Australia
Crabtree Publishing
386 Mt. Alexander Rd.
Ascot Vale (Melbourne)
VIC 3032

Contents

Heading for a Brick Wall

Picture this: a car filled with people traveling at high speed and headed directly for a solid brick wall. The outcome doesn't look very good, does it? What if someone in the car could manage to slow the car down, grab the wheel, and turn the car away from the wall? Certainly a disastrous crash would be avoided and the people in the car would be saved!

This is the message that Canadian environmental activist David Suzuki has been trying to get across for many years. Of course, he's not talking about cars. He's talking about the state of our planet Earth. He's describing what he sees as a disaster that is sure to happen if we don't start making changes in the way we live and use Earth's resources.

Getting the Message Out

David Suzuki's message has been seen and heard by millions of people across Canada and around the world. Sometimes his audience is heads of state representing any number of different countries. Sometimes it's the thousands of people who listen to his radio programs, watch his television series, or attend his lectures. His audience includes those who have read any of the more than 40 books he has written, or any of his columns or articles in newspapers or magazines. His

▲ Scientist and activist David Suzuki has been sounding the alarm of environmental crisis in every way he can for more than 40 years.

audience is also people of all ages who visit the Web site of the foundation named for him or receive his newsletters.

A Convincing Message

Although appreciation of the natural world has been part of his life since childhood, David didn't start out planning to be an environmentalist. He studied to be a zoologist specializing in genetics. He continued to work and teach in genetics even as he became more and more involved in environmental activism.

Why is David Suzuki such an effective activist? There are several reasons. He is an established scientist, researcher, and university professor. His work is based on solid scientific information. He

"I've always used the metaphor of a car. I feel we're in a car heading at a brick wall at 100 miles (160 km) an hour and everybody in the car is arguing about where they want to sit. It doesn't matter who's driving. Someone's got to say [to] put the brakes on and turn the wheel. A few of us are saying that, but we're locked in the trunk. Nobody listens to us. So we're faced with this dilemma that yes, if we hit the wall, we'll have no choice, we've got to pick up the pieces. It's a ... lot harder to pick up the pieces than to put the brakes on and start turning the wheel."

-David Suzuki

◄ David Suzuki has inspired activists across Canada. Here, young protesters demonstrate against the logging of old growth trees for the timber industry in Vancouver, British Columbia.

A Jolt of Reality

David often uses real world examples to illustrate his message. Once, on a smoggy day, he took a film crew to a hospital emergency room. There they filmed numerous children and elderly people who were seeking treatment for severe breathing problems. Many of the patients had been driven there in SUVs, thereby contributing to their own medical problems. David explained that they were so used to living in a world with serious environmental issues that it didn't occur to them that their lifestyle was connected to their illnesses.

knows how to put difficult scientific concepts into words that everyone can understand. He is passionate about the message he wants to get across. Put these qualities together, and you have a man who is able to communicate factual scientific knowledge directly and persuasively to a wide audience. What a rare combination of gifts!

Some Important Points

It takes time and experience to get to know nature well. David often points out that most people don't spend enough time outdoors where they can explore, observe, and experience nature. In Canada and the United States, more than 80 percent of the population lives in cities. Even though most people have parks or wilderness areas within reach, they spend little, if any, time exploring and observing. As a result, many people

▶ Studies show that air pollution is behind increased levels of asthma in children. In Canada the number of children suffering from asthma had risen from 2.5 percent in 1978, to 11.2 percent of children in 1995.

6

don't really understand how plants, animals, and nonliving parts of the environment all work together as ecosystems. They don't see the connection between ecosystems and a healthy, balanced planet. David points out that separation from nature results in poor decisions about the environment.

Over time, David has changed the advice he gives. He used to tell people to "think globally and act locally." Eventually he realized that this approach caused people to feel overwhelmed with an enormous sense of responsibility. Then they'd feel hopeless and give up, deciding that it was too late to do anything about it. He offers different advice now: "A lot of people doing little things can make huge changes." Along with this advice, he provides practical approaches that anyone can do to help planet Earth, bit by bit.

"[David Suzuki] has seeped into the minds of virtually every one of the 31 million Canadians... He is the environmental conscience of the people."

– Joseph R. Foy, campaign director for Western Canada Wilderness Committee, a conservation group

◄ Increasing demand for fossil fuels affects the environment and its inhabitants, such as these caribou (left, top), in many different ways. The Trans-Alaska pipeline stretches across the state for 800 miles (1,300 km). It crosses vast areas of wilderness, including three mountain ranges and more than 800 rivers and streams. Construction, maintenance, and simply the pipeline's presence affect every ecosystem along the way.

Chapter 2

Childhood: Changes and Challenges

David Takayoshi Suzuki and his twin sister Marcia were born in Vancouver, British Columbia, on March 24, 1936. They were the oldest children of Setsu and Kaoru Carr Suzuki, who were also both born in Vancouver.

Immigrant Grandparents

Both sets of David's grandparents came to Canada from Japan at the end of the nineteenth century. They were hoping for a better life. Along with thousands of other Japanese immigrants, they had been struggling with extreme poverty in Japan. To them, Canada looked like a land of opportunity and plenty. Even so, they still thought of Japan as their home, and they planned to return once they had made their fortune. They worked hard and lived simply in cramped housing, saving every bit of money they could.

Japanese immigrants were treated very poorly. It didn't get any better for their children, even though they were born in Canada. Laws were passed to keep the Japanese from voting, buying land, or enrolling in universities. David's grandparents had left a land of hardship to follow their dreams. Sadly, they found hard lives of a different kind. They worked hard

▲ Japanese immigrants found themselves in a new and strange world. Nearly everything about the culture was different, including language, dress, and food. Many immigrants, including David's grandparents, looked forward to the day when they could return to Japan.

and were able to put aside money, but they were treated with contempt and prejudice.

David's parents married in 1934 during the Great Depression. They survived by hard work and relying upon their extended family. Both had completed high school, which was a very good education at the time. In spite of having to deal with the bigotry, they considered themselves to be fully Canadian. They spoke Japanese and English fluently and had many non-Japanese friends. The Suzukis ran a laundry and dry-cleaning business in Vancouver. Their home was several rooms behind the shop.

David's Family

Marcia, David's twin sister, was sickly when she was born. Even though she was frail, her parents treated her the same as David and later, her younger sisters. At times, David thought that they were being too hard on Marcia, but their mother was determined that Marcia would grow up to be tough and able to take care of herself. She did!

The next sister, Aiko, was born in 1937. She was mischievous, independent, and artistic. David says that Aiko was his teacher in many ways.

David's father was a dreamer who was always interested in other people and what they might have to say. David and his father

▲ Japanese immigrants worked hard to be successful in their new country. Many started family businesses. This couple is running a lunch counter, where they cooked and served Japanese dishes. David's family ran a laundry and dry-cleaning business.

Internment

After the attack on Pearl Harbor by Japan in 1941, people were afraid of more attacks. In both Canada and the United States, people of Japanese descent were thought to be a threat to national security. Fishermen and other ethnic Japanese living or working near the West Coast were often suspected of being spies. First, their fishing boats were not allowed to operate. Then ethnic Japanese men between the ages of 18 and 45 who lived within a 100-mile- (160-km-) wide strip along the coast were sent to labor camps. A month or so later, all other ethnic Japanese were ordered to relocation centers or internment camps. Those who were unwilling to go were threatened with deportation.

were great pals. Together they went on camping and fishing expeditions, creating many happy memories. David describes his father as "my inspiration, my hero, my model." As a boy, David stood by the steam press as his father pressed shirts and pants, firing off question after question. In his youth, his father had read his way through an entire set of the multi-volume *Book of Knowledge* encyclopedia. All that information came in handy to answer young David's steady stream of questions.

His mother must have been a very patient woman! David loved to roam in nearby forests and streams. He often returned from his excursions soaking wet and covered with mud. She never scolded him, but she was always interested in all the treasures he brought home—insects, salamander eggs, and turtles—even though it made extra work for her. She even put up with jars of earthworms in the refrigerator and the occasional escapees that fell into the vegetable drawer.

► Japanese Americans living on the West Coast of the United States were also interned. Here, anxious to show their loyalty to their country, Japanese American citizens on their way to an internment camp flash "victory" signs, and one young boy waves an American flag.

War

David's happy childhood came to an abrupt end in 1941 with the bombing of Pearl Harbor. Even though the attack was on the United States, Canada passed the War Measures Act in 1942, depriving all Japanese citizens of their rights. David's father was sent to a labor camp and put to work to build the Trans-Canada highway. The government took over their home and business and sold them both. David, his mother, and his sisters were sent to an internment camp at Slocan City in the central part of British Columbia.

Life in Slocan City

Slocan City was a ghost town, built during the silver rush of the 1890s and then abandoned. The family lived in one room of a decaying hotel. In spite of the situation, the first year was a wonderful one for David. The rivers and forests of Slocan Valley teemed with life. There was no school during his first year, and he was free to explore.

During the time in Slocan City, David's youngest sister, Dawn, was born. Eventually, a school was built, and seven-year-old David began first grade. He found that he loved it, and by the end of the year, he had skipped to the fourth grade.

At the end of the war, the internees were given the choice of either renouncing their Canadian citizenship and returning to Japan, or resettling east of the Rockies. The Suzukis

NOTICE TO ALL JAPANESE PERSONS AND PERSONS OF JAPANESE RACIAL ORIGIN

TAKE NOTICE that under Orders Nos. 21, 22, 23 and 24 of the British Columbia Security Commission, the following areas were made prohibited areas to all persons of the Japanese race:—

LULU ISLAND (including Steveston)
SEA ISLAND
EBURNE
MARPOLE
DISTRICT OF QUEENSBOROUGH
CITY OF NEW WESTMINSTER
SAPPERTON
BURQUITLAM
PORT MOODY
IOCO
PORT COQUITLAM
MAILLARDVILLE
FRASER MILLS

AND FURTHER TAKE NOTICE that any person of the Japanese race found within any of the said prohibited areas without a written permit from the British Columbia Security Commission or the Royal Canadian Mounted Police shall be liable to the penalties provided under Order in Council P.C. 1665.

AUSTIN C. TAYLOR,
Chairman,
British Columbia Security Commission

▲ When World War II began, people in both the United States and Canada were afraid that residents of the same nationality as the enemy might be a threat to security. This notice was posted in British Columbia, Canada, to tell people of Japanese ancestry that they were prohibited from going into certain towns and other areas without a permit.

▶ Even though David's family were Canadian citizens, they were sent to this internment camp in Slocan City, British Columbia. The building under construction in the center is the school that David attended, although it didn't open until he had been there a year.

were one of the few families in Slocan City who chose to remain in Canada. Now, on top of all they had suffered because of prejudice, they were shunned and called "dogs" by people who had been their friends and neighbors. For David, the combination of the internment experience and the bigotry of the Canadian culture at the time brought about a lifelong sense of isolation. It also caused him to be more aware of, and to identify with, other minority groups.

New Home in Ontario

Resettlement meant starting completely over in Ontario, halfway across the continent from home, and living in poverty. At age 11, David worked with his mother on daily 11-hour shifts picking fruit. Eventually his parents found work in a dry cleaning plant.

▲ ▶ (Top) A view of the Slocan Valley as it looks today. It is still home to a rich assortment of wildlife, including the black bear and bald eagle (right).

David's uncles had gone east before the war and formed a construction company in London, Ontario. In time, David's family moved there too, and his parents began working for Suzuki Brothers Construction Company. When David wasn't attending school, he found new areas to explore at Point Pelee and a nearby marsh.

Although David's family had many friends who were not Japanese, dating was a different matter. His father wouldn't allow him to date any girl whose background wasn't Japanese. Unfortunately, there weren't too many Japanese girls in London, Ontario, at that time, so his father said he could also date Chinese Canadian girls. Not many of

An Advocate for Others

David's experiences of internment and racial bias have affected him throughout his life. As a college student in the United States, he backed Dr. Martin Luther King, Jr. and African Americans in their fight for equal rights. He joined and became active with the NAACP (National Association for the Advancement of Colored People) during his time as a researcher at Oak Ridge National Laboratory in Tennessee during the 1960s. After he returned to Canada, he became a director of the Canadian Civil Liberties Union and the British Columbia Civil Liberties Society. He and his family are longtime friends of, and advocates for, the First Nations people of British Columbia. They have received the high honor of being given Haida names and adopted into the clan.

them lived near David, either. His father again relented, allowing him to date First Nations (Native) girls and eventually, a black girl—all of them, of course, members of minority groups. David's high school sweetheart was Joane Sunahara, "the prettiest Japanese girl in London [Ontario]," whom he asked to a New Year's Eve dance. When they went off to college, they agreed to go their separate ways, but promised to stay in touch.

Looking Back at Early Experiences

During his high school years, David worked as a framer, building the skeleton-like framework of new houses. Later, he noted that although the framework was essential, it didn't show when the house was finished. He compares this to the way our early experiences go with us through our lives, even though others may not be able to see them. In this way, David's early experiences with racism and the injustice of internment have stayed with him and influenced him throughout his life.

Training for the Future

David's father strongly encouraged him to take up public speaking. In the Japanese culture of politeness, people were reluctant to speak out or stand up for their ideas. In contrast, in the Canadian culture, it was admirable to be outspoken. David's father knew that as a member of a racial minority, David would have to be twice as good at whatever he did as the people around him. So, he began entering David in public speaking competitions. Every night after dinner, he drilled David to perfection. First, David had to write out his speeches. Then, he practiced the speech with his father, over and over. If he made a mistake, he had to begin again. Often he ended up in tears of frustration and rage.

In time, it all paid off. During his college years, David was required to make scientific presentations to students and faculty. Not only did he receive top marks, he also discovered that he had a knack for presenting complicated scientific concepts in such a way that his audience understood and even became excited about what he was saying. He realized that he liked teaching and was good at it.

Senior Class President

In his senior year, a friend encouraged David to run for class president. David said no. He figured that since he definitely wasn't part of the "in" crowd, he'd lose. His father was furious, asking how he could be so sure that he'd lose if he didn't even try. There's nothing wrong with trying and losing, he told his son. There's no shame in not coming in first. So, David and his friends campaigned as "outies" (members of the "out" crowd). To his amazement, he won with more votes than all the other candidates combined! He learned a powerful lesson that would affect him and his work for the rest of his life: there are more "outies" than "innies," and together they have power.

◄ The training David's father gave him has served him well in his role as a powerful and persuasive public speaker. Over the years, he has continued to use the same memorization process to prepare for his broadcasts and speeches.

Chapter 3

College and Graduate School Years

There was no question about David going to college, but it was assumed that he would go to a Canadian school. Instead, a former high-school classmate talked him into applying to an American college, Amherst, in central Massachusetts. Not only was he accepted, he was also given scholarship help. College-bound Canadian students received one more year of preparation than American students did. David had always been an outstanding student, so with his record and that extra year, he thought that college would be a breeze. He was wrong! He soon found that he needed to develop better study habits, improve his writing skills, and learn the finer points of doing research. Looking back, he said that he was grateful for the way his college years shaped and reinforced his academic skills. He said, "For the first time in my life, I…[was] immersed with students who challenged me to excel in reaching for new ideas."

A Change of Plans

At first, David planned to become a doctor. Then, halfway through college, he became intrigued with genetics, the science of genes and heredity. He remembers it this way:

▲ In 1953, these two scientists, James Watson and Francis Crick, discovered the structure of DNA, the molecule that carries genetic information. Their exciting discovery opened the door to working with genes and making changes in DNA. In college, David learned about their work and was so intrigued by this rapidly advancing field that he changed his course of study.

"I sat in a class completely enthralled, my mouth hanging open in astonishment at the beauty of the insights."

Genetics was a relatively new field full of exciting questions and discoveries. Scientists were just beginning to understand about DNA, and the resulting advances reached into every area of life science. David's enthusiasm led to doing honors-level research into lives of fruit flies, and a lifelong interest in genetics was firmly established.

His parents weren't quite as thrilled with this change in direction. In fact, his mother was rather upset. Why would anyone give up a career in medicine to study fruit flies? He said that his interest in teaching began when he was able to explain his research to his parents and get them to see the importance of studying genetics.

▼ For David, Rachel Carson's book *Silent Spring* was a turning point and an awakening that would grow into zealousness. She, too, used excellent communication skills (through her writing) to give people scientific information in a way that moved and inspired them.

An Attention Getter

In 1962, biologist and author Rachel Carson published the book *Silent Spring*. This bestseller exposed some of the long-term dangers of pesticide use. The name comes from the tale of a fictitious town's "silent spring" after pesticides killed both the insects and the birds that fed upon them. The author spelled out the dangers of long-term effects of various pesticides on all kinds of life, including humans. She also offered suggestions for some possible alternatives to pesticide use.

At the time that *Silent Spring* was written, many people thought of pesticides as a good thing. After all, pesticides kept insects from destroying crops. As a result, farms could produce more food of better quality. Most people didn't realize that these chemicals could cause such harm to other living things and to the environment. Rachel Carson made a strong, reasonable argument that all possible effects needed to be considered before pesticides were approved or used. Her argument caught the attention of governments, industries, and the public, including David Suzuki.

▶ The common fruit fly is an ideal organism for genetic research. Fruit flies reproduce rapidly. A female can lay more than 800 eggs in her lifetime, and a generation is only about ten days long.

Solving a Problem

After reading *Silent Spring*, David applied his research to a non-pesticide solution. Using genetic engineering, he bred fruit flies that died in hot weather. These flies were released to mate with regular fruit flies. Their offspring would die in the heat, reducing the population and, in time, the damage they caused.

On to Graduate School

In 1958, David graduated with an honors degree in biology. He was the first person in his family to graduate from college. He didn't stop there. He went on to the University of Chicago, where in just three years, he earned a Ph.D. in zoology, specializing in genetics.

Looking back at his graduate school days, David said that he and his geneticist colleagues were "pretty puffed up" about the importance of their work in this new and exciting field. In fact, they were rather arrogant, thinking that they were superior to those who studied traditional sciences such as ecology. Now he realizes how important ecological understanding is to issues in all areas of science.

Remember Joane, David's high school sweetheart? As promised, they stayed in touch while they were in college. They got married a few months after graduation. Their daughter Tamiko was born in 1960.

Chapter 4

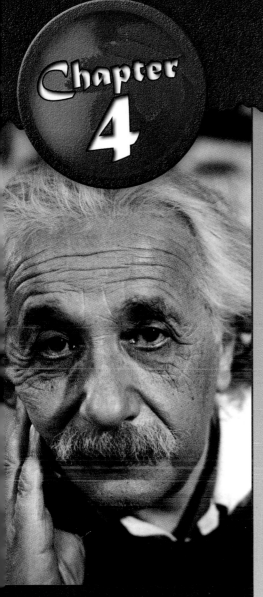

▲ When famed physicist Albert Einstein worked at Oak Ridge National Laboratory, he was part of a scientific team that developed the atomic bomb. David's field was biology, but like Einstein, he understood science as a force that could do both good and harm.

The next few years saw David, Joane, and Tamiko hopscotch from one location, and career, to another. The first move, in 1961, was to Oak Ridge National Laboratory in Tennessee. During World War II, Oak Ridge had been the site of the top-secret Manhattan Project and the development of the atom bomb. Now, nearly 20 years later, Oak Ridge was focused on biology, and David had his first full-time job, as a research associate working with chromosomes. His colleagues were some of the best-known genetic scientists of the time.

David loved his work and gained confidence in his own abilities as a scientist, but he was deeply distressed by racism in Tennessee and other areas of the South. He, too, felt separated from the culture around him. Even though he was offered continuing work at Oak Ridge, in 1962 he and his family returned to Canada. David accepted a teaching position as assistant professor in the Genetics Department at the University of Alberta. He was delighted with the opportunities to do research. Often he would work in the lab until 3:00 a.m. The cold winter was a different story.

▶ In 1964, David was invited to teach a course at the University of California in Berkeley. In his words, he went looking like a square. He returned looking like a hippie with granny glasses, mustache and beard, bellbottom pants, long hair, and a headband.

When the temperature plunged to minus 40 degrees Fahrenheit (minus 40 degrees Celsius), he decided that he never wanted to be that cold again!

When a position opened up at the University of British Columbia (UBC) for the following year, David eagerly applied for it. It meant a cut in pay, but it also meant that he would once again be able to live in his beloved (and warmer) British Columbia. He remained at UBC for the next 30 years. During this time he ran the biggest genetics lab in Canada. He also co-authored a genetic textbook: *An Introduction to Genetic Analysis*. This text is still widely in use today.

Long Hours of Research Take Their Toll

Although he was ambitious and determined, David's goal wasn't money or power. He was passionate about his research and wanted to gain the approval of the genetics scientists he admired. He worked day and night, evenings and weekends. He was surrounded by colleagues and students but isolated from everyone else. Such dedication to his lab was hard on David's family, which now included son Troy, born in 1962. David would come home in the evening for dinner and some time with his children, but then he would return to the lab. In 1964, soon after the birth of daughter Laura, David and Joane separated.

A Disturbing Discovery

Until David began teaching, his focus was the sort of research that led to new discoveries. As he prepared his coursework, he began to study the history of genetics. He was devastated to discover that genetics had been used to support the same bigotry he had struggled with his whole life. Statements made by geneticists were quoted to support laws that were discriminatory. Genetics had been used to back up the claim that some ethnic groups were superior to others. David began to dig into social and ethical issues such as genetic engineering. He knew that he had to speak out against potential misuses of genetics. It was a lonely place to be.

In 1971, David went to Ottawa, Ontario, to give a lecture at Carlton University. The room was packed with students. As he began to speak,

▶ The idea that some people were genetically superior while others were genetically inferior was not a new one. The children arriving on the train in this 1942 photo had been classified by Nazi authorities as "racially desirable." They were taken from their families in Yugoslavia and placed in children's homes or with foster parents. There they would be indoctrinated with Nazi beliefs. In his work with genetics and genetic engineering, David saw the potential for such misuse. Recalling his family's difficult experience with bigotry, he was determined to speak out against any such misinterpretation he might find.

he noticed a beautiful blond woman sitting near the front. At the end of the talk, she came down to the front with some others to continue the discussion. He really wanted to meet her, so he announced to the group that he hoped they would all come to a party that night. She did, and that's how he met his future wife, Tara Cullis. They went out to dinner that same night, but both were so smitten that they were practically speechless!

At the time, Tara was a student at the university, working on a Master's degree in literature. She had seen David on television some time before and even then had been attracted to him. She came to the lecture that day because she, too, was from British Columbia, and she was homesick. They began dating, and exactly a year later, he proposed. They were married in 1973.

David's three children were an important part of his and Tara's lives, but they wanted to have children together too. In 1980, daughter Severn was born, followed in 1983 by her sister Sarika.

Chapter 5

A Voice for the Planet: Media Activism

B ack in 1954, when David left for college, he had never seen a television. Later, he remembered sitting in his uncle's living room, watching shadows of images and electronic "snow." He wasn't much interested in the programs, but he was fascinated by the technology. Even so, he was much too busy in college and graduate school even to think about watching TV.

Beginnings of a TV Personality

By the time David arrived in Alberta in 1962, TV was an established form of communication. A local TV station had a program called *Your University Speaks*. The episodes featured university professors lecturing on their area of expertise and showing slides. David, who had quickly earned a reputation as a good speaker, was invited to give a talk. He did well enough that he was asked back to give seven more talks.

The following year, at the University of British Columbia, he was again asked to appear on several programs. By now he was very interested in the use of TV as a way to communicate. He proposed a series that would look at topics in "cutting-edge science"—new and exciting discoveries

▲ David Suzuki was quick to realize that taking science out of the lab and using TV and other forms of media was the best way to spread the word.

23

▶ Some of David's fellow scientists were not happy about his appearance. They felt that, with his shoulder-length hair and hippie clothes, he had no business representing science!

and ideas. The show was named *Suzuki on Science*. Beginning in 1969, it was broadcast across Canada. It was the first time that David was on national television, but it was far from the last.

New National Series—TV and Radio

In 1974, CBC (Canadian Broadcasting Corporation) TV began a new show called *Science Magazine*. It consisted of half-hour-long reports on topics in science, technology, and medicine. The producer knew of David's work on *Suzuki on Science* and hired him to be the host of the new program. It drew a large audience and was a huge hit. David took a leave of absence from UBC so that he could do the program. In spite of its popularity, the show was dropped after the first year. The viewers objected so strongly that it was reinstated and ran for four more years.

During the first year of *Science Magazine* on TV, the executive producer of CBC Radio attended one of David's speeches at the University of Toronto. She had already proposed a new science radio program, *Quirks and Quarks*. She hired David to host it, beginning in 1975. For the next four years, David hosted both the radio and the television programs.

The Nature of Things

Another very successful television program, *The Nature of Things*, had been running since 1960. In 1979, it was redesigned and expanded. David left both his radio and TV programs to become the new host. The show was now called *The Nature of Things with David Suzuki*. David had particularly enjoyed radio work. He was reluctant to give up *Quirks and Quarks*, but he knew that the television program would have greater impact. Even so, he was pleased that *Quirks and Quarks* continued to thrive under other hosts.

 The Nature of Things has now run continuously for about 50 years. In 2000, it was

The Danger of Taking a Stand

Quirks and Quarks dealt with a variety of issues. Some were related to David's work, such as modern genetics and advances in medical care. Others programs dealt with political issues, including race, the peace movement, and nuclear weapons. Environmental issues, such as pollution, mining, and clear-cut logging, proved to be some of the hottest issues.

 Sometimes David's stand brought danger to him and his family. After he spoke out against logging practices, his office was broken into and he was shot at. Once, when he was out jogging, a car ran him off the road and into a ditch.

◄ Clear-cutting is a logging practice in which all the trees in the area are cut down and removed. It does far more than harvest the wood. It destroys the entire ecosystem. The plants and animals dependent on the forest habitat can no longer survive there. Clear-cutting is as devastating to an ecosystem as a volcanic eruption or a fire.

voted the number one Canadian program, according to a national survey. Although the program has changed a bit with the times, it continues to take up the challenge of dealing with controversial topics. It is often the first to bring up a new subject area, well ahead of the general press. Most of all, it makes the topics understandable and interesting to its viewers across a wide range of ages, stages of life, races, and cultural backgrounds.

One Good Program Leads to Another

By now, David was becoming increasingly well known as a scientist/TV host. The fact that he was actually a practicing scientist set him apart from other hosts. Audiences liked his easy and effective way of explaining things. They also responded to the diversity and depth of the topics he presented. It's not surprising that he was in demand to do miniseries, documentaries, and lectures. He appeared not only on CBC, but also on PBS

▶ In 1982, *The Nature of Things* presented a program called "Windy Bay." It focused on the Queen Charlotte Islands off the coast of British Columbia and raised awareness of the destruction of the West Coast rain forest. Six years later, the area became part of the new Gwaii Haanas National Park, which is also a Haida Indian historic site. Over the years, the series included several more programs highlighting the region.

◄ In 1987, *The Nature of Things* presented "Nuclear Power: The Hot Debate," exploring safety issues surrounding nuclear power. The world was still reeling from the devastating 1986 explosion at the Chernobyl nuclear power plant in Ukraine. The program was scheduled to be rebroadcast in 1989, but CBC pulled it and replaced it with a show about the Arctic. The media questioned why it had been done. The result was an even hotter debate! Eventually the program was rebroadcast with a debate added onto the end of the program.

▼ The abandoned city of Pripyat is close to the Chernobyl power plant.

(United States), BBC (Britain), and the Discovery Channel, which is seen in many countries.

Several of David's programs are particularly noteworthy. In 1985, he hosted *A Planet for the Taking*, an eight-part series for CBC. In this series, David showed how people's increasing understanding of science and technology has provided many benefits, but not without a down side. A desire for material things has caused people to damage and destroy the environment to get what they want. People have put their faith in scientists to fix what is wrong, but that isn't the answer. People need to do what they can to help. For this thought-provoking series, David received the United Nations Environment Program Medal.

To prepare for one of his radio broadcasts, David spent four months traveling around the world. He interviewed scientists and other environmental experts. He asked each one: What will the world look like in 50 years if we continue

▶ ▼ In 1989, the program "Amazonia: The Road to the End of the Forest" was shown on *The Nature of Things*. Many viewers were shocked to see the widespread devastation (right). The program did a great deal to raise public awareness of the seriousness and importance of rain forest destruction. The destruction of rain forest habitat threatens the survival of such animals as the jaguar (above), the scarlet macaw (bottom), and the howler monkey (below).

to do what we are doing? The result was *It's a Matter of Survival*, which aired in 1989. David recognized the crisis and sounded an alarm. The warning was about even more than the destruction of natural systems that support life on our planet. The destruction was taking place at a terrifying rate and on a very large scale.

A Memorable Debate

In the same year, David faced Dr. Philippe Rushton, a psychology professor, on live TV. Dr. Rushton believed that intelligence and other traits were directly related to racial background. David exploded, saying, "This is NOT science!" He added that Rushton's ideas shouldn't even rate a public debate. Furthermore, he strongly suggested that Rushton be fired from teaching at a university!

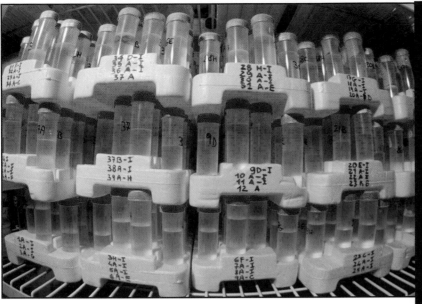

Test tubes containing the entire human genome in a laboratory refrigerator. Racks of yellow-capped tubes are seen each with a specific label. Each tube contains a particular region of the DNA (Deoxyribonucleic Acid) found on any one of the 48 chromosomes from a human cell. These fragments have been cloned and stored. Taken as a whole, these tubes contain all the DNA found in a human cell, and can therefore be called a human gene bank. Gene banks are commonly used during the human genome project, which aims to identify and map all human genes. The work on the human genome began in the late 1980s, and was completed in 2003.

More Topics for More Documentaries

In 1994, a fascinating five-part series was produced for science classes across North America. It was called *The Brain* and was hosted by David Suzuki. The series explored the mystery of how the human brain works. It highlighted the different portions of the brain and their functions. It also showed how the brain can sometimes heal itself, or compensate after being damaged.

In 1995, programs called *The Secret of Life* on PBS and *Cracking the Code* on BBC were praised internationally. The topic was the effects of scientists' ability to "crack the genetic code" and learn which genes do what. People have become better at treating inherited diseases, but this progress comes with ethical challenges. *Newsweek* magazine called this program the "first sign of intelligent life in the television season."

Returning to radio, David hosted another noteworthy eight-part documentary series:

▲ Greenpeace demonstrators hold a petition signed by one million people. It calls for labeling food products obtained from animals fed with GMOs (genetically modified organisms). Genetic modification is so common that most people eat genetically modified food without realizing it. Those in favor say it's not much different than cross-breeding, so it's natural and safe. Others, including David, say it's not natural because the traits are designed, not inherited. Unlike nature, genetic modification can transfer genes from one species to another. David points out that when the crops that result are growing in the real world, we don't know what effect they will have on ecosystems—or on us.

From Naked Ape to Superspecies (1999). Along with Holly Dressel, he described how society has tried to make Earth work the way they want it to, regardless of the damage people cause. David and Holly also said that it's not too late to change directions, and they introduced several people who were fighting back.

The Sacred Balance (2001), a four-part miniseries, was filmed on five continents. It is described as celebrating a new scientific worldview. Through interviews with a diverse group of people, David showed how humans are connected to all the life processes on Earth. He said that doing this program brought fundamental environmental issues into sharp focus for him.

As was true with many of David's programs, *The Sacred Balance* was developed into a book. It became the number one bestseller in Canada and Australia and continues to sell well.

Fame, and with It, Gratitude
With a record like this, it's no wonder that millions of people recognize David's face and

voice. Furthermore, he's right near the top of the list of admired and influential Canadians. The nature-loving geneticist, who once expressed surprise at his growing fame, has become known around the world as a voice for environmentalism.

As David looks back at the beginnings of his media activism, he's grateful for the grants he was awarded. This support made it possible for him to continue his research and do broadcasts at the same time. He has pointed out that there are two kinds of well-known environmentalists: those who are academic researchers and those who are activists. David has managed to be both.

He is glad to have been able to help so many people to think about their relationship with planet Earth and to make changes in the way they live. He says that he wishes politicians would do more of what he asks them to do, but at least they can't ignore him. They know that voters watch and listen to David Suzuki's programs!

"You're awed first by the splendor, by the beauty of the planet. And then you look down, and you realize that this one planet is the only thing we have."
- Julie Payette talking on the TV show *The Sacred Balance.* Julie was a Space Shuttle astronaut with the Canadian Space Agency.

"And that, quite simply, is the issue. We live in a finite world with finite resources. Although it may sometimes seem quite big, earth is really very small—a tiny blue and green oasis of life in a cold universe.
- David Suzuki

Chapter 6

Founding a Foundation

Over the years, millions of people had heard or read David's message. Thousands had written to him to ask, "What can I do?" Until he did the interviews for *It's a Matter of Survival*, he'd tell the people who wrote that he was just a messenger. He thought his role was to tell people about the environmental crisis that was already happening. He'd add that he didn't have all the solutions. Looking back, he realized that he was resisting the idea of being responsible for solutions.

Making a Difference

A turning point came when David's wife Tara pointed out that they had been warning people about the environment for years. Clearly they'd gotten the attention of a lot of people. Now these people were feeling helpless and wanted to do something, but they didn't know how. What could they do that would make a difference? It was time to do more than explain environmental issues and give warnings about the consequences. They needed to start talking about solutions—where to start, what could be done, and who needed to do it.

David knew she was right. Along with informing people (and alarming them), they

▲ The David Suzuki Foundation encourages us all to express how we feel about nature through writing or art. This sculpture of planet Earth in Washington, D.C., has been created from plastic bottles and other trash.

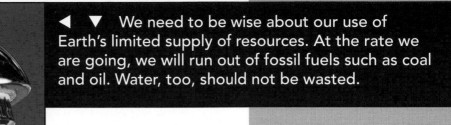

◀ ▼ We need to be wise about our use of Earth's limited supply of resources. At the rate we are going, we will run out of fossil fuels such as coal and oil. Water, too, should not be wasted.

"Nature is our home. And just as we take care of our house, we also must take care of nature. But nature takes care of us too. Nature cleans our air and water, makes the soil that grows our food and provides the resources to make all our material goods. Unfortunately, with six billion of us now living under one roof, we are gradually eroding the services nature provides— even though we depend on them for our quality of life and our future."

- David Suzuki Foundation Web site

had the responsibility to suggest ways to deal with the problems.

Is There a Need?

That's when the idea for the David Suzuki Foundation began. The first step was to gather people who shared their commitment to environmental issues but who represented different points of view. Together they discussed and debated two important questions. Is there a need for yet another environmental organization? If so, what would its focus be, and how would it differ from other environmental groups?

The participants observed that most of the existing environmental groups had been formed to address a particular crisis. These crises included such issues as dangers from pesticides, factories dumping chemicals into a river, or the destruction of a habitat by clear-cut logging.

Carbon Footprint

Everyone on our planet has a carbon footprint. What does that mean? It's a measure of all the greenhouse gases that result from our individual daily activities. These gases come from our share of burning fossil fuels for electricity, transportation, and heating. They also come from manufacturing the things we use and the clothes we wear. Even the production of the food we eat contributes to our carbon footprint.

▼ So much of what we do as part of our daily lives, such as growing and preparing our food and traveling from one place to another, uses energy and increases the size of our carbon footprint.

Each of these crises, however, was part of a much bigger picture. Although the resolution of any one of these crises was a good step in the right direction, it did not bring a long-term solution that would put, and keep, a balance in the environment.

Decisions for Direction

Several decisions were made that would direct the focus of the foundation-to-be. It would address root causes of environmental problems. By doing so, they would identify steps to take that would result in real change.

The organization would be science-based, and make use of the best scientific information available. They would hire knowledgeable scientists to help write and edit the information they wanted to produce. David knew from his experience with radio and TV the importance of communication. The foundation would work to find the best ways to get their information to the public.

Over David's objections, the new foundation was named The David Suzuki Foundation. The others prevailed. David Suzuki was a name known all over Canada, and people already knew what he stood for. The founders had decided not to rely on the government for grants or other support. They hoped that the people who agreed with his point of view would help support the new foundation.

The new foundation was officially formed in 1990. David's wife, Tara, left her teaching job at Harvard to become its full-time volunteer president. The Foundation is still going strong today with more than 40,000 members. It is headquartered in Vancouver, British Columbia, Canada. Among many other things, the foundation sends out information regularly in the form of newsletters. It maintains a Web site containing a wealth of information. One feature is David Suzuki's Nature Challenge, where visitors can learn how they can make a difference by changing some of their daily habits. Like the foundation, the site reminds visitors that "a lot of people doing little things can make huge changes."

Foundation Goals

The David Suzuki Foundation works to encourage and protect the balance of nature and our quality of life. Its purpose is to educate and study ways to care for, protect, and restore the environment. It encourages individuals, communities, businesses, and governments to consider the social and environment cost every time a decision is made.

The Foundation encourages people to reach sustainability within a generation—by the year 2030. Sustainability means living within Earth's

David Suzuki's Nature Challenge For Kids

1. Turn things off. TVs, computers, and video games draw power even when they are turned off. Use power strips and turn off the strips when not in use.
2. Explore where you live. Figure out how to get around without asking someone to drive you.
3. Be an energy detective. Check for heat escaping from your home.
4. Express yourself. Write, paint, draw, or make a video, to express how you feel about nature.
5. Learn which cars and trucks use less fuel and create less pollution, and tell your family.
6. Choose one day to eat meat-free meals. Raising animals takes more water and energy than raising plants.
7. Play outside (far left). Explore the great outdoors, learn about nature, and save electricity—all at once.
8. Use kid power to get around. Walk, bike, skateboard, carpool, or take the bus.
9. Buy locally grown food (near left). Reduce pollution from food transportation.
10. Share information. Write a letter to a newspaper, or make a poster for school about what you've learned. Encourage your friends and family to take the Nature Challenge too.

The Kyoto Protocol

In 1997, representatives of countries from around the world met in Kyoto, Japan. One hundred and forty countries signed an energy agreement known as the Kyoto Protocol. Those who signed promised to decrease the amount of greenhouse gases they produced each year. In order for this to happen, they would have to make laws or rules to cut down and limit greenhouse gas emissions in their respective countries.

The Kyoto Protocol went into effect in February 2005. It lasts until 2012. Not every country who was at the meeting signed, but most that did are making an effort to comply.

Jean Chrétien, who was Canada's prime minister at the time, signed for Canada. In so doing, he gave credit to David Suzuki and his foundation for building support among Canadians. Eighty percent of all Canadians favored it, even in the oil-producing areas.

A year later, Canada pulled out of the Kyoto agreement. David continued to put pressure on the Canadian government to honor the commitment it had made.

limits by reducing and eliminating waste and pollution. It also means dealing with the causes of health and environmental problems before they occur. Working toward sustainability will improve people's own health and well-being. It will result in a healthier planet for future generations.

Achieving these goals involves everyone. Many people already do such things as recycle, drive less, and use less electricity. Governments have the authority to give people good choices. Some countries such as Sweden, Britain, and Germany have set long-term goals and are working toward them. Other countries, including the United States and Canada, can do the same or even better.

The David Suzuki Nature Challenge is on the Foundation Web site. It asks people to promise to take the simple steps David recommends. If people do, they will lighten their individual carbon footprint upon the planet. David has challenged his fellow Canadians to commit to at least three of the challenges. He hopes that a million people will make that commitment. He says, "If we can do that, we can get anyone in business and politics to sign on."

◀ These young protestors are thinking not only of themselves, but also of their children. They want their children to inherit an unpolluted Earth.

Chapter 7

Looking Toward the Future

For the last eight years before retirement, David was a professor at UBC's Sustainable Development Research Institute. He retired from UBC in 2001. His retirement did not mean stepping aside completely. He continued to concentrate on the Foundation and his broadcasts. He also served on the board of the United Nations Millennium Ecosystem Assessment.

David has become increasingly bold and outspoken about climate change issues. In February 2008, he told a crowd of 600 students that they ought to hold politicians legally accountable for ignoring the science behind climate change. He said that the politicians had committed "an intergenerational crime in the face of all the knowledge and science from over 20 years." For this, he said, the students should see if there were a legal way to throw the politicians in jail!

Teaching the Children

The camping and fishing trips of David's childhood set a course that he would follow for the rest of his life. David credits his father with inspiring his love

▲ David has always been outspoken in his views on climate change, and on those who don't keep their promises to help the planet. On a radio show in 2007, he said that Canada's leaders should be branded as "international outlaws" for going back on the promises they'd agreed to at Kyoto.

37

> *The debate is over about whether or not climate change is real. Irrefutable evidence from around the world—including extreme weather events, record temperatures, retreating glaciers, and rising sea levels—all point to the fact climate change is happening now and at rates much faster than previously thought.*

-Not everyone agrees that global warming is actually happening. This statement on the Suzuki Foundation Web site makes its stand very clear.

of nature. He continued the tradition with his own children and grandchildren. He says camping at an early age "reinforces a connection with the environment and nature that cannot be experienced in urban settings."

When David tells his grandchildren stories about his own childhood, it makes him sad that he can't take them to the places that he and his father loved so much. They have all been built over. Even the marsh he explored as a teen is now a shopping mall. Still, he's hopeful about the prospect of sustainability and the future of planet Earth. He recalls other "impossible dreams" in our history that have come to pass. "No one," he says, "has the right to say what cannot be done."

The Next Generation—A Young Activist
At age five, David and Tara's daughter Severn gathered together a group of neighborhood

▶ The contrast between the color of this polar bear and its surroundings indicates a serious problem. The bear should be blending in with its snowy habitat. Sadly, climate change is causing the polar ice caps to melt, endangering this bear and its relatives.

children. They painted a wagon with signs such as "Save Nature" and "Protect the Animals."

At nine, she joined with several friends to found ECO—Environmental Children's Organization. They were committed to learning and teaching other kids about environmental issues. Severn describes the group as a few concerned kids who wanted to make a difference. At first they weren't quite sure how to go about it. Gradually they became more involved and educated. As they addressed problems, they found that they could generate more ideas and come up with better solutions when they worked together as a group and supported each other.

In order to raise funds for their projects, they made jewelry in the shape of lizards, called "ECO-geckos." Their first missions were local. Then, reaching beyond their own community, they raised money for a water filter for a village in Malaysia.

The Girl Who Silenced the World

At age 12, Severn and the other ECO members set a large goal. They raised funds to attend the United Nations Rio de Janeiro Earth Summit in Brazil, which took place in 1992. Top-level representatives of 178 governments around the world were attending to hammer out a plan to attain sustainability in the twenty-first century.

Severn felt strongly that someone needed to speak for the children of the world who couldn't speak for themselves. She figured that there wouldn't be anyone else giving this perspective. At the end of one of the main sessions, she addressed the delegates, and gave a powerful, passionate

▲ A huge chunk of a glacier in Antarctica calves, or breaks off, into the sea. According to recent NASA satellite data, more than two trillion tons of land ice in Greenland, Antarctica, and Alaska have melted since 2003. Scientists feel that this kind of loss is a result of global warming.

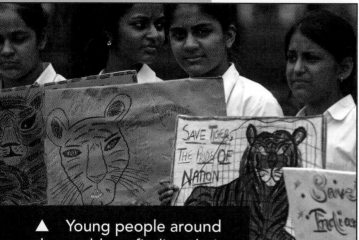

▲ Young people around the world are finding their voices to speak up with their concerns for Earth. Children in the Philippines (top) are dressed up as holiday packages to encourage people to celebrate a waste-free Christmas. These teens in India (above) are holding a rally to raise awareness of the importance of protecting tigers and the forests where they live.

speech. People were amazed that someone so young could be so knowledgeable and speak so persuasively. She was called "the girl who silenced the world for five minutes."

Later, Severn said that she was nervous giving the speech. Her legs were shaking, and she thought everyone could hear her heart beating. Still, she did it because she had to let them know that she was serious about the impact of global warming on her generation.

Severn had spent her life surrounded by environmentalists. She had learned from conversations that took place right there in her living room. In a way, she grew up living two different lives: normal school girl and environmental activist. In time, the ECO group that she and her friends began grew to become ECHO, representing the voices of children around the world.

Severn Cullis-Suzuki is an adult now. She continues to speak at schools, businesses, conferences, and international meetings. Like her father, she is a TV host and author. She is particularly passionate about encouraging young people to speak up about their future and to take individual responsibility.

From Helplessness to Hope

Severn's younger sister, Sarika, followed in her father's steps to study science. Her interests led her into advanced work in marine biology. In spite of being raised with the same childhood influences, Sarika's response was totally different from that of her sister. In her heart, she believed that the world's environmental problems could not be solved. David realized that Sarika represented many other young adults who felt hopeless and helpless. He decided to do something about it.

In 2008, David and Sarika journeyed to Europe together, along with a camera crew. As they traveled, they documented evidence of positive changes already taking place—and people who were thriving as a result. David points out when change is slow to come, it is hard for people to believe that solutions are possible. But, like Sarika, they are encouraged when they see solutions being put into action, and people living so well.

The father-daughter expedition was documented as *The Suzuki Diaries*, a special edition of *The Nature of Things*. It first aired in 2008. The documentary gave a glimpse of what a sustainable future might look like.

Denmark Eco Towns

Denmark has taken huge strides to get away from its dependence upon fossil fuels. A well-designed series of wind-powered turbines (like those shown below, left) generate much of its electricity. In Copenhagen, the capital city, bicycles are the favorite means of transportation (below, right). Every day, hundreds of people dressed for work crisscross the city along a network of paths that keep them totally away from automobile traffic.

David's daughter Sarika noted how healthy and fit everyone looked. She compared it to her own experience of bicycling in Vancouver, dodging cars and breathing exhaust fumes. "When you see it in action," she reflects, "it's all so obvious."

David Suzuki Honors

- Order of Canada Officer (Canada's most prestigious award)
- Order of Canada Companion (upgrade)
- Royal Society of Canada
- UNESCO Kalinga Prize for Science
- United Nations Environmental Medal for *A Planet for the Taking*
- Royal Band Achievement Award
- Global 500
- Order of British Columbia
- Nominated as one of top 10 Greatest Canadians by viewers of CBC
- More than 20 honorary degrees in United States, Canada, and Australia
- E.W.R. Steacie Memorial Fellowship for the outstanding research scientist in Canada under the age of 35
- Four Gemini awards (best host of a Canadian TV series) and an ACTRA award for work on *The Nature of Things*
- John Drainie Award for broadcasting excellence
- Fellow, AAAS (American Association for the Advancement of Science)
- Bradford Washburn Award, Museum of Science, Boston
- Lindbergh Award from the Charles A. and Anne Morrow Lindbergh Foundation

It showed that sustainability really is possible if people—governments, organizations, and individuals—are willing to make it their goal. It gave believable evidence that living a sustainable lifestyle does not mean giving up quality of life.

An advertisement for *The Suzuki Diaries* described it this way: "A father who wants to pass on a better world...A daughter ready to embrace her father's legacy." David has passed on that legacy to millions of people: those who have watched and listened to his broadcasts, read his books and articles, signed and followed his nature challenges, and, above all, thought seriously about his message. He insists that sustainability is possible, and that each person can make a difference.

▲ Environmentalist David Suzuki smiles as he is invested as a companion into the Order of Canada at a ceremony in Ottawa, Friday December 15, 2006.

Chronology

1936	Born in Vancouver, BC, Canada
1940	First fishing trip with father to Loon Lake
1942	Father sent to labor camp in Solsqua, B.C.; family sent to internment camp, Slocan City
1945	Suzuki family released; relocated to Ontario
1954	Graduates high school; enters Amherst College
1957	Attends first genetics class; changed direction of life
1958	Graduates from Amherst with honors BA in biology
1958	Marries first wife Joane
1961	Ph.D. in zoology from University of Chicago
1961–1962	Research associate at Oak Ridge National Laboratory, Tennessee
1962	First broadcasts: *Your University Speaks*
1962–1963	Assistant Professor in Genetics at University of Alberta
1963–1993	Professor of Zoology (genetics) at University of British Columbia
1965	Marriage to Joane breaks up after birth of third child
1969	Full professor at UBC; ran biggest genetics lab in Canada
c. 1993	Professor at UBC's Sustainable Development Research Institute
1971	Hosts first CBC show: *Suzuki on Science*
1972	Marries Dr. Tara Cullis
1972	Awarded E.W.R. Steacie Memorial Fellowship (three years)
1974–1979	Hosts *Science Magazine* on CBC
1975	Beginning of CBC radio program *Quirks and Quarks*
1977	Invested into Order of Canada (high honor)
1979	Begins hosting *The Nature of Things with David Suzuki*
1985	Hosts eight-part CBC TV series *A Planet for the Taking*
1989	Honor: given name "Nuuchee" by Nuu' Chah' Nulth First Nation, Tofino, B.C.
1990	Co-founds (with wife Tara Cullis) the David Suzuki Foundation
1992	Addresses Earth Summit Conference in Rio de Janeiro, as does 12-year-old daughter Severn
2001	Retires from teaching at UBC to focus on environmental causes
2007	Cross-Canada tour to speak to Canadians about climate change
2007	Along with Al Gore, speaks at Youth Summit on Climate Change
2008	Travels to Europe with daughter Sarika; produces *The Suzuki Diaries*

Glossary

activist A person who works actively and publicly to bring about change

advocate A person who speaks on behalf of another person or group of people

bigotry The state of mind of someone who stubbornly hates and shows prejudice and intolerance toward members of another race or ethnic group

colleagues Associates; people who work together in a profession

controversial Causing an argument or debate because of opposing opinions

deportation The removal of a person or people from a country

DNA (Deoxyribonucleic acid) Hereditary material found in humans and most other organisms. DNA molecules inside cells carry genetic information and pass it from one generation to the next

documentary A work such as a film or television program that presents information in a factual, informative manner

ecology The study of the relationships between organisms and their environment

ecosystem A community of organisms and the physical environment in which they live, interacting together as a unit

environment The combination of living and nonliving factors that surround and influence the growth, development, and survival of organisms

ethical Done according to standards for right conduct or practice

ethnic Relating to people sharing a common origin, heritage, culture, or language

fellowship An award of money given to support a graduate student or researcher while doing additional research or getting more training or experience

First Nations The Native people who have been living in North America before and since the Europeans came; particularly those who live or have lived in present-day Canada

fossil fuels Carbon-rich fuels such as coal, oil, and natural gas formed from the remains of ancient plants and animals

foundation An organization established for a specific purpose and funded by contributions

genetic engineering A technique in which genetic material, especially DNA, is cut, spliced, rearranged, and reinserted into an organism to change one or more of its characteristics

Great Depression A period of widespread economic hardship in Canada, the United States, and other nations during the 1930s

greenhouse gases Gases such as carbon dioxide, methane, and nitrous oxide that trap heat in Earth's atmosphere

irrefutable Proven; absolutely certain beyond any doubt

metaphor A figure of speech in which two unrelated things are compared, for example, "The election was a landslide"

NAACP The National Association for the Advancement of Colored People—an organization begun in 1909 to promote the rights of African Americans

pollution Substances that make areas of the environment dirty or harmful

protocol A detailed plan or set of steps to be followed in a procedure, experiment, or intervention

quark A very tiny particle of matter that makes up protons and neutrons

quirk A peculiar trait or odd habit

recycle To use something again; to alter something so that it can be used again

scholarship A grant or payment made to a student, based on academic performance, financial need, or some other reason

smog (smoke + fog) Visible air pollution that forms a brownish-yellow haze

zoologist A scientist who specializes in the branch of biology dealing with animals

Further Information

Books

Cherry, Lynne, and Gary Braasch. *How We Know What We Know About Our Changing Climate: Scientists and Kids Explore Global Warming.* Dawn Publications, 2008.

David, Laurie, and Cambria Gordon. *Down-to-Earth Guide to Global Warming.* Orchard Books, 2007.

Suzuki, David, and David Boyd. *David Suzuki's Green Guide.* Greystone Books, 2008.

Thornhill, Jan. *This is My Planet: the Kids' Guide to Global Warming.* Maple Tree Press, 2007.

Woodward, John, and Jennifer Skancke, editors. *Current Controversies— Conserving the Environment.* Greenhaven Press, 2006.

Web sites

www.cbc.ca/documentaries/natureofthings/
This official Web site of the CBC program *The Nature of Things* contains a wealth of information about current and future broadcasts, including overviews and guides, interviews, profiles, newsletters, and interactive features. The episodes can be viewed online—a terrific resource especially for those who cannot watch the program at home.

www.davidsuzuki.org/
The Web site of the David Suzuki Foundation posts the most current environmental news and events. It offers suggestions for what people can do to help and provides information-packed articles about many of the most pressing issues.

www.davidsuzuki.org/kids/
This section of the David Suzuki Foundation Web site is especially for kids. It contains David's Nature Challenge for kids plus activities, some very cool links, and test your knowledge quizzes.

www.epa.gov/students/
This is the student center home page of the EPA (Environmental Protection Agency) site. It offers information, activities, projects, and more. It's a good place to look for notices about environmental award competitions, scholarships, internships, and careers.

Index

48

About the Author
Suzy Gazlay is an award-winning teacher and writer of children's nonfiction books. She has also developed educational curriculum and frequently serves as a content consultant.